RISE unstoppable

ISBN-13: 9780985552749 (paper)
ISBN-13: 9780985552756 (eBook)

Edited by Eva Xan
Illustrations by Attabiera German
Cover Designed by Mark Hobbs

RISE unstoppable

Michelle G. Stradford

Also, By Michelle G. Stradford

I'm Rising: Determined. Confident. Powerful

When Love Rises

DEAR READER

"Rise Unstoppable" is book three in my "Rising" poetry series, written to celebrate the tenacity and the capacity we all possess to transform and rise to be an unstoppable force.

The themes in this collection focus on the self-created barriers we place on ourselves, and the trauma of unhealthy relationships, including sexual and physical harm. This book also touches on the social and racial injustices that many of us face, as well as the challenges and biases we often address in navigating our work lives.

In these pages, I offer my thoughts on self-love, personal care, healing, and growth in the face of the obstacles, and trauma life sends our way. While I do not claim expertise, I have learned a few lessons along life's adventure that I am eager to share. I hope you find my poetic prose, affirmations, and verse relatable, and come away with an existential, and lasting experience.

DEDICATION

This book is dedicated to Keith, my husband, and soulmate. You are my rock, and compass through the wall of the storm, leading me back to my center when I lose the way. Your unwavering encouragement and support calms and sustains me. I am grateful to have you as my life partner. I love you.

TABLE OF CONTENTS

Painting with my heart,
I pour my soul
on to life's canvas.
Storytelling is my art.
These words are my paint.
I gift them to you,
and pray they leave
an indelible imprint.

Imprint

SELF-CARE

She tugged firmly
on a thin thread
of faith
untied herself,
just let go,
and released her fear
of unraveling.

She watched
herself unspool,
her magic
unfolding into
infinite potential.

Unravel

I will not direct
this rage, born from
trauma and shame,
upon myself.

Instead, I will
forge anger and pain
into a hardened shield,
that protects
and fortifies me.

Fortify

There is a riot
ravaging my heart,
threatening
to take me down,
and burn it all
to the ground.
I'm in a fierce fight
to regain control,
will not be
overcome
by your grip, and
ever-tightening
hold.

My Riot

Our most salient
deep-rooted memories
latch on to us,
never allowing
all the good to fade
entirely away.
They transcend the bad,
allowing our minds
to sink the sorrow.

That moment when
we rose above it all,
cannot evade our hold.
Only the positive
remains ingrained
so that we continue on.

We seek the beauty
in our tragedy,
life's sacred lessons
so, we can bear
the tears, untold pain,
and withstand
the unimaginable.

Beauty in Tragedy

I revel in this
languid hour,
my place of refuge,
a moment of quiet
to hold me still.
My sparkling glass
is half-full,
as my mind strolls
into summer chill.

With weary feet
nesting in pillows
on the teak chaise,
I dry a French pedicure,
and bask my cares
in the low orange light
of warm sun rays.

This is a fitting finish
to an elongated week,
an action filled day.
Alone with my thoughts
nothing more to slay,
I toast to my dreams,
life, and the cosmos.
I celebrate me
guilt-free.

Guilt Free

My fragility
humanizes me,
magnifies
my womanly
powers.

I will not allow
you to use it
to weaken
or reduce me
to a wilting flower.

Magnify

I am not
my mistakes.
They only
made me stronger,
smarter.

I am newly
sharpened, shaped
by the lessons
I have learned,
missteps,
wrong turns.

No, I am
better than them.
Still growing
and flourishing,
I'm just an
evolving human.

Not My Mistakes

**I wake inside
of an uneasy feeling,
rough, unsettled,
just off, like a day
with no end,
without limits.**

**Head wide open
and sky-less,
exposed, like an
unfinished room
empty and bare.
No one's here
to claim me,
make me their home…**

At times I get
wedged into spaces,
and pull at my
raggedy edges.
I've misplaced my roar,
no fire left in me,
to burn off
these burdens.

Somedays, I just
need to be a face
with no name,
when all I want,
is to be left alone
to search…
for a new reason,
to mend these holes
that have riddled me
and left me soulless.

Soulless

**Stop feeding
your anxiety
with unfounded beliefs,
wasted promises,
and obnoxious people,
that leave an aftertaste.**

**Filling you with
negativity, they
offer nothing of value
no real substance,
causing inflammation,
that breeds stress.**

**Starve your angst
with solitude.
Cleanse the waste
from your mind and life
for a balanced, fulfilled
and healthier you.**

Starve Angst

**I nurse my pain,
and go on despite
the bruising losses.**

**Grateful I am
granted a chance
to wipe my slate clean,
I set about winning,
earning my way
to champion again.**

**My talent remains
abundant,
utter determination,
and laser focus
is still intact.**

**With a little grace,
and earnest hard work,
I will bounce back.**

Bounce Back

Sometimes
there is no way
to will her way out
of life's oppressions,
even as she strike's back
against the troubles
and callous people
who assail her.

She watches helplessly
as her sun continues
to slide off the edge
of the world,
fading into the horizon
off to oblivion,
shredding her world
in to ribbons
of depression.

At times, it is hard
to impart,
state her needs without
nearly falling apart.
But she is mightily lifted
by an assuring whisper
or gentle hand
on her shoulder.

A kind unspoken gesture
is what she needed
to take that next step.
It inspired her to get up
and keep on going,
dig herself out
from the wreck.

With a little help,
she believed
she would find
her way back,
reconnect, and get
freshly committed
to growing stronger.

Gestures

When life knocks
over your paint,
makes a mockery
of your mistakes,
resist rushing in
to correct, and instantly
clean up the spill.

Allow your colors
the room to flow,
blend together
just run wild.

Let magic take hold,
transform you,
change your canvas.
Watch the juxtaposition
of the out of control
render you
into a stunning
work of art.

Spilled Paint

**Never ignore your sparks,
the hardwired responses
and gut feeling.
Embrace, and own those
uncontrollable reflexes,
the ones triggering
your hypersensitive
anger; the uneasy.**

**They are your fuses,
designed to be
the weak link,
and put you on alert.
They're meant to fail,
shut things down,
contain the damage
and prevent an explosion
from spreading,
torching you, like wildfire.**

**Just blow, let out
the pent-up frustration.
Lash out in anger.
Unleash your feisty,
the surging spunk.
Your fuse is designed
to protect you.**

Short Fuse

There are places
in my past I dare not go.
I fear I could never
find my way back
through life's
trapped doors.

Trapped Doors

Heart butchered open,
dragged through life
with more than
an ego bruised.
My twisted arms,
and precious parts
of me that were broken
all eventually heal.

But the traumatizing
theft of self-worth,
failure to protect
my personhood
from dehumanizing
hurts, people who
were never good,
is a near-impossible
mountain to face.

How do I begin
the climb, return,
and regain my own
collapse of self-trust?

Recovery

I was traveling
in the right direction
until you jumped in,
attempted a takeover,
undermined my choices,
tried to co-opt my life.

I refuse to allow
you to seize my spirit.
I embrace challenge,
am not in fear of it.
I will decide, own the
actions to take.

I determine what I require
of myself to expand,
bend and not break,
but excel and achieve
untold growth.

I will plot my success
and invest in my future.
Just stop meddling.

My Success

You spun another
web of empty excuses
to justify your
unsavory behavior.

Pledging to undo
the damage,
you'd begged me
to forgive you for,
"Just believe and
leap with faith,"
you said.

**When you took leave
of your senses,
went on the run,
your absence
stunned and
took everything
in me not to
come undone.**

**I blocked, ejected,
and exiled you
to protect me
from your abusive
cruelty and idiocy.
No, I do not accept
your false apologies.**

False Apology

No longer a puppet,
I stopped pretending
trying to imitate
a made-for-you
authentic life.
I released the pent-up
bitterness,
power washed away
your sickening
protectionism,
yes, finally tasted
the salt in my rain.

The cleansing,
overdue self-forgiveness
felt good, and freed me.
All of my trials,
long stoic years,
built-up the agility
to make a move.

No longer crippled by,
dependent on you,
I can finally utter
a coherent sentence
without your
menace in my head,
or your crooked
hands up my back.

Not a Puppet

It is futile to try
to grow a thriving life
inside of a lie.
Plant your future
in truths that frighten,
and tremble you with
excitement.

Truth

Resist the need
to wear your
cloak of strength
anywhere you go,
suiting up
for every battle.

Stop trying to face
challenges alone.
You do not have to
always be the lone one,
the leader in charge,
the only tough one.

Put your
alpha-drive on pause,
give it a break,
and yourself some rest.
Emerge from your respite,
strong and replenished,
mentally prepared
to win the fight.

Take a Respite

State what you require,
then find, learn,
and earn it.

Decide to
borrow or buy.
Just give it to yourself.

No person will
take care of
or fulfill your desires
better than you can.

Name your need, then
stake your claim.

Name It

I ended my habit
of hanging on to
self-limiting behaviors,
hoarding hurts,
nursing cuts from
broken relationships,
repeatedly trying
to fix them, and me.

No more turning
friendships off,
then feigning interest
again in dead-end
conversations
or toying with outdated,
and obtuse ideas.

I'm done trying on
overblown and outgrown
images of me,
over and over again,
knowing they
never originally fit.

Habit Ending

**Sometimes,
I want to run
back in time,
to catch my tears,
and cup them
inside my hands.**

**I wish I could
hug and reclaim
myself,
before I had to learn
how to tie knots
in the sheets
to keep me
out of reach.**

**At times,
I wonder what
could have become
of the sparkles spun
by that wide-eyed,
in awe of the world
dimple-cheeked,
five-year-old girl.**

Reclaim

Select a
captivating word,
then close your eyes.
Now fixate
on a peaceful,
sublime state.

Dance to the
songs of nature,
listen to them
sounding off
each other,
sent to serenade.

Set the mood free.
Let it roam around
inside your daydream.
Watch it leap,
travel to places
you dared not go__
no, never believed
you belonged.

Let it linger,
and knead out
the stress,
coax away
the phantoms
that can no longer
hurt you.

Reverie Word

I know that
stockpiling
the relics of a
former existence
threatens my future.

Still, I save away
torn-off pieces of me,
the shaming, and
unconquered fears
I could not shake.

I gather up
discarded dreams,
dropped, left behind
and all the chances
I failed to take.

I lower my head
in dismay,
looking misty-eyed
upon these remnants
of what used to be.

Then I fold them up,
carefully saving away
for the right time
when I can cease
hoarding faded memories
and am readied
to restart living.

Hoarding

Tonight, I am
drunk on bitter,
bent over in a thick
sorrowful stupor,
lapping it up thirstily.
I'm one with pain.

My lips tremble
as this ache makes
its way through me,
pilfering my lungs,
screaming out anguish,
pain coagulating,
and strangling my veins.

I watch them flow
out over my skin,
as tears come in waves,
cleansing, and numbing.
I'm unable to quell
the stabbing jabs
as my chest swells.

I wail, writhe
until I collapse limply.
At last, I lay still,
my sobs running dry.
For in the morrow,
it will all end.
I refuse to cry
this same
heartache again.

Same Heartache

**Doubling down on
your own needs
is not a luxury,
it's a psychological
self-care necessity.
Make yourself
the top priority,
always number one
on the list.**

**Keep your fire fed,
burning hot, and bright
so, you can dial up
your heat at will,
be a shining beacon
in the night
to those you love
who depend on,
and need
you the most.**

You First

In a sudden start,
I open my eyes,
heart hammering
against my chest,
warning me to flee.
I try to process
the dark blur
coming into focus,
crawling and creeping
onto my twin bed.

I push away
the rough hands
grabbing, touching,
smothering me,
but am pinned
beneath his stench.
I struggle,
breathe through
the pockets
of stale, hot breath.

The smell of abuse…
It never leaves you__
not even after the
thousandth day
I've scrubbed my skin,
to rid, wash
my body of him.

I attempted__
time and again,
to tell of his sins
until days led to years.
But a child's mind
could never
find the words
for what he did.

Tonight and
everyday,
I will his face
to implode, disappear
from my memory
to stop haunting
my psyche.

Like a broken bone,
the ache found
a home; it returns
to taunt me at will,
raking my resolve
across tiny
shards of truths,
breaking open
unhealed wounds
that I suffocate on.

Suffocate

Taking time
for yourself
barely qualifies as
minimum self-care.
It is an essential
responsibility,
a requirement
for the permit to carry
your womankind
membership card.

Woman Care

**Re-opening old wounds
drowns me every time.
Submerged face-up,
I struggle and gasp for air
under this fresh pain
rushing, grabbing at me
from the nightmare
that never ends.**

**It is finally time
that I uncover,
and slice this hurt
back open,
pull the folds wide,
force the poison-infested
thoughts out into the air,
lay bare it all
to fully heal.**

Wounds

Release yourself
from the bondage
of unhealed scars.
Allow your butterflies
to return and hover.
Feel them flutter.

Let the excitement
in again to accelerate
your mending
and restore you
to your original wonder.

Original Wonder

She sleepwalked
through blue days
in search of a corner
to fold herself into,
and meld with
the background.

In need of a power down,
to be disconnected,
she retreated,
surrendered, let go
of the stifling energy.

Now drained
completely discharged,
she returns sublime,
muscles loosened,
mind and spirit quieted,
restored, rested
and ready
for a full recharge.

Restorative

"Not allowed" is
an inflammatory
dark ages mindset,
a throwback phrase
that can get you ejected.
I own my choices.

The path I take,
life-forwarding decisions
or colossal mistakes
are of my choosing
and my journey to make.

Either way, I will not bow
or let you dictate
what I finally allow.

I Allow

The woman who
you once knew
ceases to exist.
That one who
could not resist
your stories, greedily
swallowed whole
each lie you fed me.

I once denied my
complicity when you
were stealing
my hope away
and hijacking my bravery.

I no longer believe
that you'd never again
betray my trust
or lay heavy hands
on my skin.

Yeah, she has exited,
left the premises,
and is no longer
accessible.

Inaccessible

Leave the comfort
of your perch.
Leap out of the nest.
Use your wings.

They not only make
you a fantastic force,
and give you flight,
wings grant you the
freedom to transcend.

Use Your Wings

We are broken
from the brutal beatings,
being held down,
shut out, redlined
and locked up.

Tired of drowning
in our own tears
as you look away,
and rinse the blood
from your hands,
sanctify your mind,
ridding yourself
completely
of any culpability.

The harsh reality
that no one
is coming to save us
seeps into our lungs.
siphoning oxygen,
deflating optimism.
It drains hope from our brains,
sending us in circles
of emotional paralysis.

We have been
suffocating for over
four hundred years.
This free-ish rope
never stopped strangling
and suspending us
in subhuman
subsistence.

We sadly watch
you step over black and
brown bodies, murdered
at the hands of brutality
choosing not to see
our free spirits dying,
gutted of hope.

Our protests are neutralized,
outcries teargassed
as you normalize
slow-motion genocide
of a once majestic people
with your silence.

Let Us Breathe

My fruit lay
bruised and hardened.
It was plucked way
too soon.

What would I
have ripened into
had I been left
alone to bloom?

Bloom

You have set the bar
far too low,
by repeatedly excusing
their shortcomings,
and rewarding them
with shiny stars,
praise kisses,
and sexual favor accolades
for barely meeting
the basic expectations
of a monogamous
commitment.

Hold yourself accountable
for that which you aspire;
the love you deserve,
the respect you require
and all you strive for.
Put them to the test.
Demand the best
by raising your bar.

Raise Your Bar

Just stop playing
the victim.
Refuse to engage
in blaming.
Reject all forms
of self-shaming.

It's time to pivot
and get back
to building
the best you,
by resetting
and prioritizing
your life goals.

Exorcise the
weak and fragile
mindset.
You're better
than that.

Not a Victim

In a moment of clarity,
I ruthlessly set fire
to the chaos
in my cluttered life.

I cleared away
years of debris,
cutting relationships
that had siphoned off
all my energy,
darkened my outlook,
and dimmed my light.

Now I see more clearly,
have regained lost time.
I claimed back the space
to still my mind.

I found the perfect fit
for my misplaced parts
and freed up a place
inside of my heart
meant only for me.

Only for Me

There is healing
in facing our pain.
But my bag of agony
was too hurtful
and toxic to unpack.

I had to let it go,
just leave behind
the baggage
too heavy to carry.

I taught myself
to forget,
and purposely
lose things.

I let go of the people
I had mistakenly
believed to be treasures
so, I could finally fly.

Unpack

**Self-acceptance
of your quirks,
imperfections,
unique perspective
should not be your
license to give up.**

**Don't ever grant
yourself permission
to quit on you.
Never stop the work.**

**Keep fine-tuning
and improving
to shape and chisel
the best you.**

Never Stop

TRANSFORM

Oftentimes, a reckless
moment from the past
or recent transgression
clings to you
like double-sided
adhesive folded back
upon itself.

Despite how delicate
you work to peel
the wrongs away,
you cannot pull
the pieces apart,
nor make them
right again.

You'll never break
completely free
without tearing
and ripping off
the unhealthy
parts of you.
Growth is painful.

Adhesive

Turn off the noise.
Shut out those
loud negative voices.
Brace yourself
for the fractures.

If parts of you break,
new growth will replace
what was weak
and has become obsolete.

This storm that came
to shake you
was also meant
to water and replenish.

It was sent to reshape,
forge and change
you and me for the better.

This hardship was meant
to stand you upright,
making you more
reliable and stronger.

It will place you
in the right position
to do the thing
you were made for;
to forge through
this test of all times
to attain higher.

Higher

I stumbled forward,
striking out
in all directions,
letting myself down.

Yes, too many times
I got drunk on promises,
and blindly followed.
I strained to keep the pace,
permitting myself to be
pulled along, apart.

Straying too far,
I gasped for air.
Finally, I recognized
the liberating
power of choice
and rose in rebellion.

I yanked on the chain,
let go of the leash,
and halted
my runaway train.

Let the Leash Go

Following directions
blindly down
a straight path
because you were
unable to choose
your way
can lead you in circles,
take you on a
never-ending
journey to nothingness.

Know where you
are going.
Steer your own
navigation.

Navigation

When your world
is spinning out,
self-doubt can take
a vise-hold on you__
The support you'd
counted on has fallen away,
friends are nowhere
to be found__

Remind your
frightened girl
that she can't exist
in your bold woman
just-get-it-done world.
You have risen
far higher than
your shortcomings,
and have grown
stronger than anyone
through harsh
life challenges.

You are responsible
to nurture your
self-confidence,
and grow the courage
to believe in you
even when all you have
is hope to cling to.

Grow the Courage

Stop losing
your will
in the "woulds."
Create an abundance
of "could"
so that you
find yourself
among
a collection of "dids."

The Woulds

Hear me, see me.
Try to understand
my idyllic
perspectives,
distinct experiences,
and pre-dispositions
before labeling me
bitter and angry.
Or attempt to dismiss
my existence
altogether.

My authenticity
is the best thing
I can offer.
If we are both willing
to sit, listen, and truly
care to know what
is important to each other,
together, we can form
a deeper connection,
stake claim on
honest discourse.

Authenticity

**Are you built solid,
strong enough
to withstand
my full force,
be my fail-proof
tested safety net?**

**Can I count on you
to vault forward,
dive to keep me
from falling?
Will I break you
as you reach, trying
to catch save me?**

Strong Enough

**Sometimes your rain
does not just roll in
for a momentary
torrential downpour,
or even a daily shower.**

**Like a tropical
depression, it stalls,
regains strength
then sustains itself
on chaos, hot winds
holding your life
in a mind-numbing
gray hover,
not for days, but years.**

Dreams wash out
in flash floods,
casting doubt over
bright futures,
delaying goals
yet-to-be attained.

Your sun hides behind
the protection of shadows,
seemingly lost
forever to the underside,
masked in perpetual
dark clouds.

Then, the blue skies,
like an old friend,
suddenly appear
out your window.

Nothing remains
permanent, not even
the torrential rains
that have watered
your seeds for years.

Watered Seeds

Singled out
and uprooted,
snatched away
from your grounding,
just a surly weed
that's overgrown.
Believed invasive,
and treated
like a nuisance,
you were unvalued,
the one never seen.

You hold on,
struggle to fight
for life,
though isolated,
separated
from the light,
your source
of sustenance.

**Feeling lost is
expected,
but fleeting
when adjusting
to most new things.
Slow down,
and explore,
don't try so hard
to acclimate.**

**You will discover
a warm and
fertile place
that is receptive,
and welcoming__
the perfect plot
to plant new roots,
grow a healthier you.**

Rooted

You relinquished
the right to helplessness
when you outgrew
your adolescent ways,
the formative years,
those long-forgotten days.

Stop expecting,
waiting for sheer
magic to just happen
and for someone to appear,
move you to action
or show you their "how."

There will never be
another intersection
with choices like this.
This perfect juxtaposition
and you were meant to exist
in the same universe,
where moments like this
are meant to be born.
Today is your now__
Yours to claim, and own.

Your Now

Is your ethos
enduring, anchored
deeply rooted
in non-negotiable
beliefs?

Are you tenuous,
easily changeable,
always morphing
to mirror the trend?

Is how others
view you,
believe they
know you
consistent
or ever-changing?

Solid Ethos

Just quit with
the self-effacing
diminishing,
I am not worthy
comparison bullshit.

Stop wilting.
You can withstand
the heat.
Recall the fire
you walked through
to get here.

Stop Wilting

When lost amidst
the madness,
I hold fast to all
that motivates me,
embodies my reason
for being, living.
I look to what
keeps me grounded.

At the end
of the maze
I'm confident
I will discover
that I was never lost,
only in need of a pause.

I stop for a moment
of clarity
to hone my direction
and retune my
inner compass.

Inner Compass

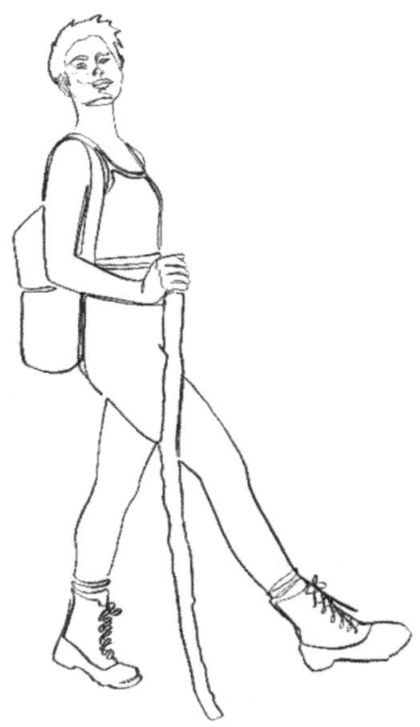

Is your lifeline
anchored securely,
and built with multiple
levels of redundancy?
Does it depend on
consistent healthy
life-affirming practices?

Is it wound tightly with
thick threads of integrity,
and solid beliefs?
Or is it woven with strong
all weather faces
who will stand
by you, with you
no matter the failure?

Has a higher power
covered it in faith?
Is it made from
the sturdiest ropes
forming a tight web
to hold your weight
should you stumble,
trip or free-fall?

Check Your Lifeline

Do not be known only
in the past tense.
Avoid being defined
in terms of "I used to be this"
and "I once did that."

Never allow your history
to eclipse the present you.
Own your narrative.
Stay active, relevant.

Create a new version
by writing your
re-imagined story.
Yes, create a refreshed
present tense you.

Present Tense

Consistently
sheltered from harm,
she nearly collapsed
under intense pressure,
and the unbearable
temperatures.
When her protection
was lost, she could
barely function
on her own.

She ventured from
the cover of others,
gained exposure
to some heat
and stepped up to take on
the hard challenges.
She stopped fearing the fire,
didn't cower at the harsh light
and risked a bit more each day.

Finally toughened,
she adapted, learning to
withstand life's burns
now that her shelter
was long gone.

Exposure

Hold on tightly to your
confidences
until you determine
whether people
are ready to experience
the real you.

Some are ill-equipped
and can't handle
your essence,
raw truth.
Others will
never be worthy…

Not for Everyone

Not obtaining
that one thing
you have worked
so hard towards,
long-hoped
and prayed for,
can be a blessing
or the best outcome.

Be mindful of
and grateful for
the near misses,
almost, could haves,
the hardships
avoided.

Your decisions not to
may have saved you
from a sad reality
or event which
could have tragically
finished you.

Near Misses

No one has to tell you
being born black
makes you a threat,
target or guilty
of an unnamed sin.

Your mind slowly
gathers up the clues:
the slights and glares
on the playground.
Being followed,
stopped and detained
repeatedly as a teen.

Denied homes, loans,
jobs you earned
your way to,
because you don't
look like *them*
and wouldn't "fit in".
Repeatedly referred
to as slurs, being called
a nigger to your face.

The oppression,
***it* grows in silence,**
like a sinister
cancer for years
creeping, spreading,
taking hold.

Then you awake
one day
feeling less than,
and dispirited,
like a light
permanently
switched to dim.
Your humanity stolen,
pilfered right out
from under your skin.

Stolen Humanity

When a voice truly
touches, speaks to you,
finds a way to reach
through multiple channels…

When it's annoyingly
persistent, stubborn,
always showing up
at times most inconvenient…

When it consistently infuses
your consciousness
with unexpected
messages and wisdom…

Be silent and cease denying.
No more resisting.
Sit still, and just listen
to hear, understand your vision.

Just Listen

I am trapped
inside of this hell,
chained and twisted
into intricate knots,
fighting to retrieve
the remains
of my dignity.

Defending who
I *in fact* am
without being
misunderstood, viewed
as a militant victim
touting a fake identity.

I was lured here
by the layers of lies
constantly fed to me,
of the wide-open freedom,
and a grand life
of equality,
only to be denied
the right to my own
personhood.

Faux Freedom

When your reservoir
runs low and empty,
close your eyes,
and summon visions
of what has always remained
most important to you.
Picture the faces
of those who motivate
and move you,
rotate your world.

Revisit the places
that slow your heartbeats,
chase gloom away,
keeps your lonely at bay.

Fill up on fond
remembrances,
life affirming moments
that can never be lost.
If you bank on
all of these
emotional riches,
you will soon be
made whole again.

Made Whole

No more discarding
my unfinished parts,
or erasing, hiding
and painting over
my unsavory art.

I found the courage
to accept and integrate
my differences.

I treasure the best of me,
am refining the rest.
My full portrait is emerging,
depicting my best.

I am an original creation,
a colorful masterpiece
in the making.

Masterpiece

Real change
requires discomfort,
a complete teardown,
and a masterplan.

Strip away mindsets,
practices and beliefs
that no longer align
with your values.

Recover your fortitude.
Hold on firmly
to unwavering optimism.

Gather up the virtues
required to build
a more fulfilling life.

**Move forward,
and walk away
even if sacred layers
of you lay discarded
across the floor.**

**Step over what remains.
Leave behind
the heavy anchors
that long-held you down,
and anyone who works
against you,
or means you harm.**

**Complete the checklist,
for your meticulous plan.
It's your validation
that you have already
transformed.**

Transform

Wary and doubtful,
I unwisely made
adjustments
to my values.
I blurred the hardlines,
and compromised
my own absolutes,
desperate to keep you
central in my life.

I bent the rules
for your most egregious sins.
Yet, you betrayed
my deepest trusts,
violated my spirit,
and nearly left me undone.

Though you burned
holes through me,
left my soft parts charred
and hardened,
I used the ashes
to grow anew.
Now toughened up,
and newly strong,
I've cut my losses.
I had to move on.

Blurred Hardlines

AMPLIFY

I do not come by
these truths by choice,
but thru a palpable
pulsing of my spirit.
Some usher in the good,
others bring insistent
stark realities.

They permeate
color into my being,
flow like a river
to and through me,
reciting my sorrows,
playing me like music,
whispering my secrets
rhythmically to the
urgency of time.

Hard truth subsides,
like rapids breaking
inside my head.
Waves of joy rush in
lapping and flowing
over the brim
of my soul,
filling my reservoir
up with liquid poetry.

Liquid Poetry

You will exhale again.
Do not take this
pause for granted.
Revisit the primal
cries that carved
sacred messages
on to your heart,
when it soared
exuberantly with
newborn wonder.

Rest, reflect, renew.

Germinate your ideas,
allowing them to sprout
into grand plans.
Savor this time,
to grow yourself anew.
Filter out the negative
with a cleansing,
fresh and exhilarating
deep breath.

Exhilarated

Perhaps
you consider
me unpredictable,
and a paradox,
or commonplace
and unimaginative…

Be careful judging,
and dismissing
my unseen,
getting lost
in the intrigue,
ignoring the hidden.

Hardly benign
or harmless,
I embrace
my unknown,
choosing to be
an enigma.

My question mark
excites, expands,
makes me, and my world
grander.

Enigma

I prefer to be
in the company
of an enlightened man
who will not attempt
to weaken me
and make me feel
the least significant.

Instead, I stand
with those
who challenge me
to be better,
push for excellence,
offer support,
strive to make
me stronger,
not use me
like a prop, a bolster
to make them
appear smarter,
loom larger.

Enlightened Man

I was that teen
praying to God
to help me grow
round hips, a butt
standing high enough
to set a book on
and gift me
massive breasts.
Okay…just larger
than a B cup.

Only then could
I finally become
popular, even pretty,
the sought after one.
I'd have the boys
falling all over
my voluptuous body
making me date-worthy.

Good thing
she didn't listen,
forcing me to look within
to see that the values
instilled
and the intelligence
to focus on the parts of me
that truly mattered
was most important.

Instead of my dream body,
I was granted certain grace,
and bountiful blessings.
I was gifted a brain
that clung to beauty,
the classic lines
and could design spaces
where people work, play
and appreciate global cultures,
unfamiliar places.

I was inoculated with
a small solid dose
of humility
leading me to discover
and appreciate
my intrinsic beauty.

True Beauty

Be a standout leader
known for starting
something,
a staunch follower.
Perfect being the
best supporter
or effortlessly blend in.

Your choice.
Just be deliberate,
wholly committed
to whatever the path
or role you choose.

Be your own advocate,
a champion for you.
Bring your best
to the people, causes
and communities
that mean the most to you,
move you forward.

Stop waiting
or asking to be seen
or heard.
Stand up, say or
do something
to create your own
visibility, if that's
what you need.

Create Visibility

Replace the lies
you taught yourself
to believe
with daily truths
steeped in self-worth.

Write them in a note
and mouth the words
in the mirror
until you are moved
into action to escape
your self-inflicted abuse.

Replace Lies

At no time
should you hesitate
speaking gently
to the fragile,
and at risk.

Build mutual trust
by taking turns sharing,
and watch their petals
open like a flower
to caring inquiries.

Reveal a piece of you
so, they feel your
vulnerability too,
showing you have
been where they are,
that you relate,
understand them.

Commit to being
a genuine friend,
and not just
a befriended.

Not Befriended

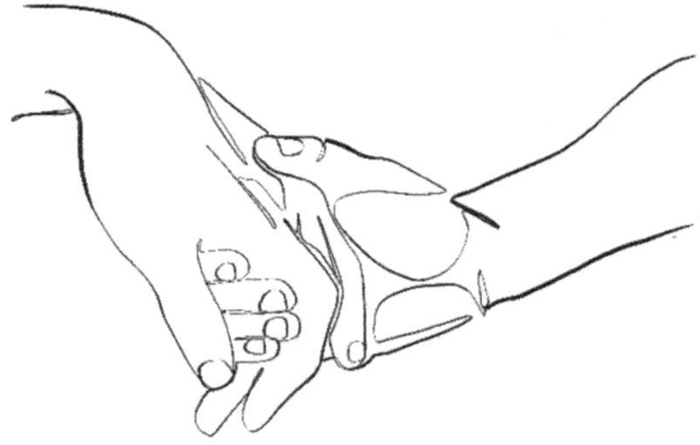

I rescued my
tattered heart
from a hostile place,
I had mistakenly
believed
accepted me.

I am relieved that
it's still intact,
and we are both
imperfectly
beautiful.

Imperfect

Inspect your smile
before you wear
it each day.

Is it contrite,
off-putting,
dimming your shine?
Or wide, warm
welcoming,
transmitting
your light?

Words always fade,
but your smile
leaves a lasting impact
on every heart
you open or forsake.

Impact Smile

Your yellow feels
reverberate
off my eardrums,
coloring the sounds
of you rushing
over to me,
splashing through
gurgling water.
Sounds of laughter
swell in stereo
swishing, stirring up
my neurons,
immersing me.

My mood rises
on the tiny bubbles
bursting in my head,
each, exploding on impact,
titillating every second,
showing me
that happiness
is not to be held,
but must flow freely
to inspire, excite,
touch and move
each other.

The love I deserve
is the difference
between simply
existing and
truly living
every day
dancing across
the sun.

I pray you feel
and experience me
as deeply as
you have moved me.

Move Me

Never fall back
when you possess
real knowledge.
Step out in front.

Live knowing
that someone else
is depending
on you to lead.

Those who have
lost their footing,
their voice
are counting on
your courage
to stand up.

Stand Up

World, I see through you
from my clear open view.
No shutter-speed
manipulation
can alter this frame.

Widening the lens
will not broaden
my perspective.
Filters won't change
or sweeten your
cruel realities.

Your inhumane injustices
complicit silence,
corrupted policies,
and supremacist racist
inhabitants
all conspire to threaten
my wellbeing, my life.

You cannot soften
your harsh light.
I cannot unsee
the untold truths
you have shown me.

World I See

Stay attuned to
the friend
whose voice falters,
who believes themselves
undeserving
of a kind word,
and would never ask
for anything.

For just a day,
take up one of their
multiple struggles
until they regroup
to regain strength.

Walk with them
on their journey,
and you'll both feel lifted,
the shared load
tremendously lighter.

Lighter Load

It is difficult
to process that
in the present day,
social missteps
unfold as if decades
of progress
has been erased.

Men and women
are equally guilty,
whether in a bank,
lecture hall or office,
in an emergency room,
construction site,
or in a cozy restaurant.

Deferring to the man__
the pervasive assuming
him to always be
the one in charge__
must end.

End Deference

Go ahead, woman up.
Own the strength
you were built on.
Your raw courage
and self-confidence
is invaluable.
Your feminine qualities,
intuitive wisdom,
and hard-earned
experience matter.

Be an advocate
for equality.
Use your voice,
influence, vote,
and leverage your power
to set a firmer foundation
for the strong women
who will inherit
your lineage.

Persist, and keep
pressing forward
until you are forged
into a woman made
indestructible.

Indestructible

Why treat yourself
with any less reverence
than the character
in a book?

Something about her
got you hooked,
made you care,
pulled you in and invested
in what happens next.

You find yourself
in her corner, rooting.
You would do anything
to see her be triumphant,
emerge a champion.

Whether granted
a few months or years,
life is no fantasy.
You are the story.
Live it like a heroine.

Like a Heroine

Don't underrate
the power of
your womanly ways.

Long-past are
the expected-to-be meek-so-
men-do-not-appear-weak days.

Command respect
for womanhood.

Womanhood

You gift me
twilight sun rays
at the bottom
of my darkest midnight,
and bright,
blissful mornings
near the end of gray
Wednesdays.

At every make-or-break
moment, you're there
ensuring I prevail,
holding me upright
never letting me fail.
You hold my face
to the light.

You are my
charmed muse,
a golden unicorn,
making me believe
I can craft magic
out of nothing.

My Muse

Believe that a woman
works as hard,
is as smart and capable
as any man.
Equality and freedom
to choose is not
a nice to have,
it is a fundamental right
as an earthborn
human.

Stop judging,
and preaching,
just end
the persecutions.
No more calling
her out for refusing
to be silenced,
or passed up,
undermined,
mistreated,
and subjected to abuse,
physical
or emotional.

Quit with the
character drag-downs,
tainted with half-truths
and steeped in outright lies.
Stop making her
out to be the
guilty until proven
pure and more worthy.
Stop telling women
that nonconsensual sex
is victimless.

You cannot know
the complexities,
all the layers
we are made of,
how any of it feels:
the internal battles,
a heart drowning
in dilemmas,
or the courage
it takes to put
ourselves out there.

You will never
feel our struggles,
walk the treacherous paths,
sip the bitter taste
of our truths
until you've been one.

Believe a Woman

Her life is
greater than
the earthly particles
her soul came cloaked in,
meant for more
than to occupy space
or reproduce life.

Her worth is
self-defined
by the essential
elements that are
intrinsically
attributable to a woman,
yet far more.

Her unique artistry,
is born of
unapologetic
transparency.

Her value is
measured by her
influence and far-reaching
impact on the lives
she touches.

Her worth is
measured by the
rate of energy
she expends creating
and sharing optimism.

She Is Invaluable

RISE

Choose carefully
with whom you
invest your seeds,
and plant your hopes.

The condition,
and value
of their lot in life
is likely deceiving,
their offering
not as fertile, or rich
with promise
as you have been
made to believe…

Rich with Promise

My goals held
no promises,
stalled out and sank,
until I learned
to fight like a woman.
I put my fearless
fortitude to work,
used my survivor's
mindset,
pushed through
tiny setbacks
and tall tragedies.

I developed
the resolve to tackle
any challenge,
and worked to make
my life more worthy
as if it would end
tomorrow.
I didn't count on anything
to be given to me,
and set about planning
every detail meticulously
to be the success
I was destined
to be.

Like a Woman

Stop trying
to adjust me.
Don't turn
my heat down
because you
are uncomfortable
and unwilling
to risk the burn.

I'm hurt and angry.
No, I'm not okay.
I am beyond
determined.

Do Not Adjust

**She took honest stock
of the cards dealt,
discarding anything
that would cause her to lose.
Then, she determined
her next move.**

**Too often discounted
and offered no support,
she watched them
underestimate
her prowess,
depth of knowledge.
Then, she maneuvered
into her killer position.**

Reposition

Her extraordinary
talents lay shrouded.
She walked tall,
yet remained invisible,
swallowing
her opinions,
fanning away
the smoke they blew,
and throttling her fire.
But her voice
would not
remain silent.

**She strode up
to the podium,
spoke emphatically,
flexed her fortitude,
and shared convictions.**

**Despite the panic
building and threatening
to wreck her senses,
she embodied
her principles.**

**Now a force,
she will not return
to being the last one
to be heard.**

Hidden Talents

There's no need for you
to clean up, put away
the messes I have made.
My chaos is ordered.
I know where to find
whatever I need.

I consistently extract
invaluable jewels
from my mistakes…
Have gained life lessons,
tough learnings from
unintended turns.

Leave my treasured
stockpiles of wisdom,
and layered pieces
from my storied life
that you seem to deem
worthless alone!

Treasure Piles

Refuse to fall
victim to defeatism,
even as the negativity
starts to gain on you.
Stay one stride out front.
Never accept
eventuality.

Reject all
possibility of losing.
Stay with your moment.
Do not let up
until someone
is walking away
with the prize,
while you strategize
to clench a win
the next time.

Reject Defeatism

**Her unknown
strength was revealed,
then excelled
when she had
no other choice
but to prevail.**

Prevail

You did not create
this dark space
and do not deserve
to hurt or feel trauma.

Just know you will find
your way back.
It takes time to grieve,
to fully heal yourself.

Keep doing the work.
Hold on with all your might
to faith, your sanity
so, you can light up tomorrow.

Healing

My will broke…
I faltered,
despite the hours,
years of chasing down
solid aspirations.
Careful plans failed
to catch the wind,
and take flight
on the timeline
I had meticulously
mapped.

I felt upended,
trapped beneath
the burden of defeat.
Yet I recovered
my resolution,
took a new position,
found an alternate way.
My goals,
undeterred fervor
were not obliterated,
simply suspended
until I was readied.

Suspended

My survival required
me to hasten my hardening,
roughen up my edges,
and grow a thickened skin.

I cured up long enough
to not just survive,
but thrive, in the face
of injustices, and lies.

The multitude of life's
challenges
have shaped, changed
and fully toughened me.

Tough-Skinned

**Beware of those
who feed their egos
by belittling women:
The sly ones who
avoid real talk,
are consistently
dismissive and incapable
of an authentic exchange,
yet poke around
your edges for a way in.
They are expert at provoking,
leaving their pinpricks
under your skin.**

They claim you make
them uncomfortable__
But no, "There is not an issue."
No conflict to address here.
Yet they profess their fear
of confronting you,
citing the unwarranted
emotions of a woman,
some phantom one,
not you specifically.

Call them out.
Put a name on it.
Never allow anyone
to deflect.
Find a way to hold
the misogynists
fully accountable
for their heresy.

Misogynist

Cautiously consume
unsolicited advice,
sugar-sweetened
and poured
from beautifully
painted
ceramic faces.

Ceramic Faces

**I cannot know
what will develop,
in this new reality,
or imagine what
will become of me
beyond today.**

**But I am prepared
for a natural evolution,
and I'm more than positive
that I will emerge
even stronger
on the other side
of this invisible enemy.**

**I stand ready to fight
and protect
for both you and me
against the risks…
Adapt to the unknown
and take on a future
clouded, shrouded in
an uncertain daze.**

Uncertain Daze

They ripped into her
and exposed her deepest hurts,
triggering unspent rage
and dangerous
silenced eruptions.

She vaulted into swift
unsuspecting strike-backs,
exacting damage
and doing untold harm
they never expected.

Fight Back

Turn down your
cynical filter,
when reality knocks
you backwards
as they constantly
pull the chair
out from under you,
all the while
gesturing that
it was meant
for him instead.

They tell you it is
not your time.

You go at it alone,
consistently left
out of the plan.
You're tired
of being told
this is not
your world,
not your home__
that you are
a valued visitor
invited to observe,
not an actual
contributor.

Keep a cool head,
listen astutely.
You are rapidly
being schooled
on the reality of hierarchy
your presumed place
in society and the economy.
Just hold that thought
for the time when
you *own* the table__
where equity
and justice will be
served up as
the only agenda.

Your Agenda

Be prepared for a
venomous response,
despite your apology,
and the decision
to fall back.

Let my poker-face
be your warning.
Even as I say,
"Oh, it's okay,"
find no safety
in my calm.

Poker Face

You have worked
tirelessly
to earn your place
and advance
to a higher level.

But success,
your mere existence
may threaten,
intimidate
those who believe that
when a woman wins
they must lose.

So, labor even harder,
show up more than ready,
three times smarter
to reach, maintain,
and defend your position.

Defense Position

Persistent pressure
over the years
produces gems.
Despite her fears,
she kept pushing,
standing firmly,
and holding on
until she created
diamonds
out of sheer force.

Her Diamonds

I just ripped apart
the staged image
of the walked-all-over girl
frozen in a still-life,
who no longer
identifies as her.

Greet the unpolished,
still emerging,
but fully capable,
rough-around-the-edges
she.

Have yourself
together
and be fully prepared
before
coming for me.

Re-Emerge

**Wiped out,
a total knockdown,
on the other side
of a tidal wave,
barely treading
but still standing.**

**You are rare,
unsinkable
and not to be taken
for granted.
You're never
to be shaken.**

**Take the risk,
do the amazing,
get back to being
remarkable again.**

Remarkable

**Whoever comes at me,
trying to block,
or hijack my mission…
I'll beat you back
with irrefutable defiance.**

**I refuse to be defined
or held down by
a chorus
of the untested,
never-risked-anything
uncourageous voices,
my staunchest
fake supporters.**

**I reject your negativity.
You have no place
in my life if you
stand against me.**

Defiant

Regain access to the place
that has always served
as your command center.

Adjust the controls.

You own the power
over how you allow
chaos to alter you.

Control the Chaos

This raw anger
belongs to me.
The suffocating,
long-suffered regret,
my pulsing pain…
It is all mine.

Remove your grip.
Stop prying it away.
Cease preaching,
projecting, telling me
that I must move on
and just get over it quick.

I never requested
that you take on
my experiences,
sensations
or my life as your own.

This is all mine
to wallow in,
handle and live through
to prove that I am
more than capable,
fully able to process
the breadth of emotions
that define me.

These volatile
reactions will increase
my resilience,
and make me stronger,
a formidable fighter.

Let go, so that
I can resolve and clean up
my own mess, grow,
and make progress.

My Progress

With nothing to lose
but my reputation,
self-respect and honor,
I speak out now
because I refuse
to have my voice erased.

I will no longer
feel alienated,
be invalidated
or made the victim
by your silence.

Not Silenced

I reject the notion
of an insipid
non-existence,
or a sticky label
affixed to me,
predestined to fail.

I will not be stripped
of my heritage,
redlined to the
grimmest of paths,
or trapped in a dead-end
all because
of the packaging
I arrived in.

Labels

She lost her way,
stalled in dead water.
The wind for her sails,
was nowhere
to be found.

There was no time
to wait for help,
or high tide to bring her in.
She held no hope
that she'd be rescued
by the rise.

Resolve kicked in,
a raw survival instinct
took hold of her hands.

Yes, she pushed
her way through it,
used what she had
and just rowed.

Just Row

Newly rejected?
Take your hard-earned
lessons and launch
those big dreams
into action.

Focus on what
you know how to do.
Revive the faith
still stirring in you
to conjure up
something mystical
out of thin air.

To actualize your goal,
become the cause,
start a personal movement.
Get past wallowing
in dejection;
it was a required
detour, a jolt to set
your re-direction.

Redirected

The sacred
touchstones
of my life,
everything
I have known
is under fire,
just gone, turned
upside down.

Once solid
foundations
suddenly shift,
breaking apart
and knocking down
firm beliefs
that buttressed me,
had held me firmly.

I bow my head
in thanks,
ask for wisdom,
then begin the crawl.
It does not
end this way
I will claw
my way back;
I can never
be stopped.

Will Not Be Ended

**Telling your story,
even to those
who are unworthy
releases the power
it holds over you.**

Your Story

Why do you keep
trying to slow me,
constantly
throwing up blocks,
stepping into
my pathway?

I am not about
to lessen me__
dull, dumb down
this sheer intensity.

Flying my highest
heights,
soaring beyond
warp speed.
I am filled up,
fueled.

Stop trying
to dim my light.
I'm aiming to be
something more,
that beacon,
a constant, roving
through the night.

No Slowing Me

I relive the
excruciating hours,
when these walls
were too tall to climb,
and felt I could not go on.
I watched useless days
limp along and collapse
into bottomless nights.

Recounting the memory
of unbelievable pain
is the only way
I am reminded
that I am alive.

New energy leaps,
reverberates
off my bones,
stirring me
up in a fervor.

I am a survivor,
a testament
to the suffering
as offered evidence
of living messy,
walking fearlessly.

I shun an orderly
existence.
My struggle,
ability to feel pain
is the proof of life.

Evidence of Life

Remain vigilant.
Do not let up on your
intensity or tenacity.
Never waver in the
face of setbacks,
or the knockdowns.

They are simply
roadblocks
sent to help you
find a way around
and take a new route.
The best lessons
and greatest blessings
come hard-learned.

The fiercest battles
are the sweetest won.
Fight for what you need.
You are way past
being worth it.

Tenacious

UNSTOPPABLE

I stand confidently.
I am the calm
in the center
of the storm,
the protection zone.

I plant my feet to brace,
shield myself from
the furious winds,
harsh threats,
and frightening unknowns.

I've steeled myself
inside the wall
of the quiet eye,
my inner sanctum,
where they lose
all power to harm me.

The Calm

Like a phoenix rising,
my butterflies are lit,
restless, pulsing,
and setting
my head ablaze.

Agitated, I clamor
to roam free,
and break out
from this cocoon.

I tore through,
smacked down,
and knocked away
my self-restraints.
Beyond ready to fly,
I'm on fire.

On Fire

**She stumbled,
landing face down,
breaking the fall
with her courage.**

**Taking stock
of everything,
she created a plan
and set aside her pride.**

**Crawling first,
she clawed away
the years,
filled up the days
with sweat and tears
never doubting.**

**Ever persistent,
she pulled herself up,
walked again,
then ran and won.
The end.**

Her Persistence Story

Stop following
your dreams.
Get out in front,
and take the wheel.

Drive them hard.

Turn it up high,
to light speed
until your
dreams lift off
and fly you.

Drive Your Dreams

I long to roam free
like a butterfly
inspiring, transforming,
just spreading
compassion.

I seek the light,
the nectar of longevity,
delivering the promise
of new life,
and a future from
one heart to another.

Owning and living up to
what I was designed for,
I do my part
to cultivate minds,
creating beauty
just for the gazing.
I treasure every second
of this short life.

Like the butterfly,
I fly unacquainted
with regret,
no worrying over
the span of my wings.

When my work is done,
I'll flutter way up high,
disperse my zest wide,
aiming boldly for the sun,
flying my most beautiful.

Fly Beautiful

I am beyond intense,
running on high octane.
Please understand
that nothing
you can do or give
will ever complete
or fill me.

I do what I must,
taking care
of my own needs.
You can run with me,
do us, or Life,
together or not.

High Octane

**Invest in yourself.
Raise the stakes.
Open up,
and lower
your defenses.
Tune your receptors
to learn from the driven.**

**Emulate the
highest achievers
and do the thing,
the work, the training
and educating,
to ensure valued life
experiences are attained.**

Do what is required
to train and ready
yourself to grow
into a fire-breathing
indefatigable dragon.

Be eager to torch goals
and light fire to the world.
Prepare to slay volatility,
inevitable roadblocks,
whatever challenge
arises that dares
to obstruct your way.

Prepare to Slay

**When your winter ends,
you will find me
blooming in the spring,
still growing
where you left me,
preparing for a
fruitful summer.**

Seeds

**Up at four o'clock A.M.,
putting on my Teflon.
I'm giving everything,
have goals to attain.
I must expand
my ambitions,
create my own thing.**

**Yes, I must realize
and achieve
all I have worked
my entire life to reach.**

**I am not out here
grinding, to merely win.
I'm ready to crush,
and annihilate.
I came to vanquish.**

Vanquish

In the presence
of an audience,
she sprints through
conversations
at dazzling speed,
never leaving time
for them to catch up
get in a word,
or finish a thought.

She leaves scarcely
a moment to engage
for interjection,
or real discourse.
Driven by the need
to remain in the lead,
she towers out front.

She holds them
all at bay, lapping
at her spiked heels.
She is winning
because she is faster,
three times as good.
She will never wait
to be heard.

On Her Heels

In the face
of indignities,
rude distractors,
the whispered slights,
hostile stares and slurs,
look your aggressor
firmly in the eyes,
then walk away.
Hold onto your grace.

Walk in Grace

This is a takeover,
I'm about to silence
the dissuaders.

I'm shutting down
anyone, anything
stalling me,
or blocking my way.

I over-plan
to drown out suspicions,
hitting with the force
of a tsunami.

I'm leaving no reason
for any questions,
or challengers
and eliminating
all doubters.

Tsunami

I parted my lips
to protest and reject
the proposition,
but your kiss
arrived first uninvited,
clearly
unrequited.

I had told you
that I was never
interested, not attracted.
You labeled us
as a disconnect,
bad timing,
saying I sent mixed signals,
"Sorry for the
misunderstanding."

Let me be clear.
I will not tolerate
another instance
of your persistent
and blatant harassment.
No need for further
discussion.

This Is Harassment

Nothing eases
my inner fears,
replenishes
my superpowers
like the knowledge
that I am
inexhaustible.

I arrived revved up,
then floored it,
giving it all I had.
I steered through
the obstacles
with a few assists,
driving myself
to the top.

No, I will not
apologize
for being here,
and I won't justify
my achievements.

There is no time
to be gracious…
I earned it.

I am getting
fired up
for my repeat.

Earned It

Self-assured,
and determined
she pushed her way
through the aftermath
of the crash,
carrying what
remained of her life.

She found a place
for shelter,
building a solid
foundation.
But the troubles,
life's new challenges,
and past dangers came
racing from behind.

They chased, caught,
threatened to consume,
and take her down.

She fought with faith
as her only shield
erupting in a blaze of fire,
She turned on her heat,
and watched them burn.

She kept pushing,
charged through
her attackers
until she reached
the other side.
Bruised, but intact
she brushed
away the ashes.

Now ablaze in light,
she is renewed,
more lethal,
and ready to ignite.

Blaze of Fire

Oxygen, cut off.
My flame blew out.
But as long
as my will
still smolders,
there is a chance
for me to re-ignite.

A Chance

I leave behind
the dark past
that once blinded
and nearly maimed me.

I refuse to allow
night's hungry
shadows to ever
consume me.

I'll keep my face
held up to the light.
I will not succumb,
shall never turn back.

Not Succumb

Stop asking for my
my nonexistent papers,
or permission to walk,
run, protest, speak out
to shop, eat, just breathe.

I won't make myself
smaller to protect me
or shield you,
from the danger
harbored in your mind.

The threats you make,
and volatility you create
by your own actions
will be your undoing.

I will not back down
to avoid escalation,
because you cannot
stand for me to be
in your presence.

I will call you out,
fight back against
your overt actions,
and challenge your
off-color opinions.

No longer will I tolerate
any of your aggressions.
I refuse to apologize
for my existence.
Your complicity
fuels my resistance.

Resistance

No longer an
injured woman,
I am a reckoning,
a red, full on
volcanic eruption.

I am a warrior,
a lone victor
in the making.

I survive, and thrive
simply because
I drank my own hype
and made myself
believe that I am
invincible.

Invincible

I will not be
overshadowed
by my failures,
or defined
by a misstep.
I will recover,
then decisively
slaughter whatever
comes next.

Cast from molten steel,
and golden lineage
that would
not be ended,
I am already
custom-made
for life's tests.
The light will find me.
I was designed
to shine.

To Shine

I can hit hard,
rocking to the core,
leap to conclusions,
ricochet out of control.
I incite you to commit
and do things
you never dreamed.

I spew geysers
of molten heat
that upheave
false assumptions,
triggering your
small explosions.

I blast wide craters
through unfair,
unjust notions.
I fill you up,
feeding you
fresh thoughts,
and a change in
perspective.

But, the frightened,
threatened minds__
they scatter far.
The betrayers remain,
trembling weakly.
With startled eyes,
they sob, fixate
and gaze at me.

I feel the pulses
throbbing out loud,
attempting to still
their silent shakes__
all the while riveted,
never registering
my magnitude
or heeding
the warnings.

I am an earthquake.
Never meant
for traitors,
or for the faint.

Earthquake

**Draw strength from
your insufferable pain,
and blinding darkness.**

**Feed it to the energy field
that hastens your heart
and excites your mind.**

**Let it move your feet,
even when weighed down,
or dragged by the weary.**

**Protect your life source,
the special magic
unique only to you.**

**The enduring power
that just won't quit
inside of you.**

Endure

**When discouraged,
she calls on
her faith
for restoration.**

**Then raises
a tall glass
of kick-ass
to amplify
her position.**

**Where she stands
is never
a question.**

No Question

My mind is lit,
can't get to sleep.
I am ignited,
and on point.
I feed fire to
my creative lion,
like it's oxygen.
I'm building
the improbable.

Bolts of light
clash in my head,
setting off possibilities.
Brilliant sounds,
and abundance
fill me with visions.

There is no
stopping this.
I am the thunder,
breathing to life
the Superwoman
I am becoming.
Yes, she does exist.

Superwoman

Pain's permanent
stains may taint
her remembrances.
Yet she rises above,
tempering
her terminal aches
with grace.

She wears disarming
naïve acceptance
on her face,
holding hard lessons,
lifetimes of breaking
deep in her heart,
and keeping
lost causes safe.

She makes loving
herself an art.
Her inner beauty
can never be lost
or defaced.
She is unforgettable,
inerasable.

Inerasable

Taking rise
and flying
untethered__
***No limit* embodies**
the dream
of every woman,
each earth-born human.
Not just for women,
rich in deepened hues
of beautiful color__
it's a rallying cry
for all who long,
need to be lifted.

It is a reminder
that you are amazing,
articulate and gifted.
Know that others
have been there
and survived the place
you are headed.

We took a similar
journey
of transformation,
changing into
and becoming
something greater.

We had to dig deep,
pull ourselves up
and out of the abyss.
We had to escape
the suffocating,
that shortened our breaths
threatening to break,
end us.

We see you, embrace,
and hold you up.
Whether you are a mother
trying to raise strong sons,
or independent, more
enlightened daughters.
Or you've been
beaten down in life,
by a soul-sucking career,
an abusive partner,
with no family to claim…

We stand here with you,
and support your next move.
Will hold you up,
celebrating each success,
praying you never stop
moving through it.
Never cease making
your rise unstoppable.

Rise Unstoppable

FROM THE AUTHOR

I am grateful that you have found your way through "Rise Unstoppable" and, hope you will come back to it when in need of a distraction from life's daily grind.

Feedback, whether a phrase, a brief sentence, or a paragraph is valued and appreciated. Your input helps me validate my themes, and informs me about what I should write next. So, please take a moment to leave a rating and review online at the retailer site where you purchased the book.

To stay updated on my next book release, read samples of work in progress, etc., please connect with me:

Instagram @michellestradfordauthor
Twitter @mgstradford
Facebook @michellestradfordauthor
Pinterest @michellestradfordauthor
Bookbub: michelle-g-stradford
Goodreads: Michelle G Stradford

Subscribe to my newsletter for book release updates, promotions, and giveaways.

Newsletter: https://geni.us/MGStradfordNewsletter

ACKNOWLEDGMENTS

Once again, I am grateful to God for blessing me with life experiences that I share in this latest collection. I thank my family for their unwavering support and encouragement as I continue to write my heart out.

My daughters Madison and Camdyn inspire me to be a better person. I am proud to be their mother and pray that my husband and I have guided them to be the best people they can be.

My journey as a writer has been enriched by the many readers who have reached out to me to share the impact my books have had on their lives. Thank you for allowing me to share in your world.

ABOUT THE AUTHOR

Michelle G. Stradford is a bestselling Author, Architect, Artist and Photographer who creates written, visual, and inhabitable art. In addition to poetry, she has written short stories and fiction since adolescence. Her writing style is contemporary free verse, as her goal is to create poetry and prose that is relatable, connects with and is inspiring to her readers.

In particular, she wants to use her experiences and writing to build a platform that encourages women and girls to own their power to overcome challenges and crush their goals. Michelle is married and has two daughters.

CHECK OUT THESE OTHER GREAT TITLES BY MICHELLE G. STRADFORD

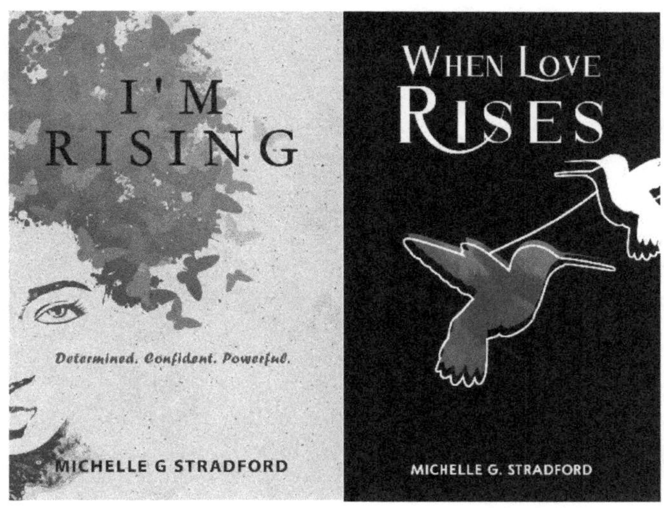

Other Books:

"I'm Rising," is a number one bestseller of powerful self-love poems and mantras about life's triumphs and tribulations.

"When Love Rises," is a poetry collection that celebrates love, offering comfort in heartbreak and inspiration to heal, move forward, and try love again.

Made in USA - Kendallville, IN
1165299_9780985552749
09.15.2020 0854